DOING BUSINESS AS UNUSUAL

Proverbs 31 Guide for Women Entrepreneurs

Doing Business God's Way Series, Book I

Doing Business As Unusual   Copywright©2017

All rights reserved. No portion of this book may be reproduced in any form or by any means without prior consent of the Author and Publisher.

Distributed by Createspace.com

Front Cover Illustration by Books by Tonya, courtesy of Google Images

Author Contact Information:

Tonya Franklin
Books by Tonya
Website: www.tonyadfranklin.com
Email: booksbytonya@gmail.com
Phone: 601-589-0676

Intro

You're a Christian. You run a business. So you're automatically a Christian business owner, right? Well, maybe you are, and maybe you're not. Have you taken a look at your business structure? Is it designed to glorify God? Is it designed to fulfill the call God placed on your life, and complete the mission He spoke over your business?

We associate Proverbs 31 to women in regards to being the perfect "wife," but have you thought about how the scriptures apply to how you are to run your business and build your brand?

Take a look at the "skeleton" of your business and perform a self-check to see if you're running your business specially designed by God… or are you doing business as usual??

Proverbs 31:10
"Who can find a virtuous woman? For her price is far above rubies." KJV

What does the word "virtuous" mean? According to the Merriam-Webster dictionary, it means having or showing high moral standards.

So what are the standards that you've set in your business? Have you ever thought about that aspect? In designing your business, you do a business plan, right? In that plan, where does God fit in? Is He merely mentioned in the executive summary, or does He flow throughout the entire plan?

Now let's define standard. It is a level that you're looking to attain. So now the deeper question is: where are you looking to get to? A ROI of 45%? Hmm, or maybe you're looking to get that new house you were praying about a mile outside of town?

When setting standards for your business, there is nothing wrong with setting physical objectives and goals, but also set spirituals ones. Build your brand spiritually.

The scripture says that her price is far above rubies. A ruby is considered to be an extremely expensive gemstone. In biblical times, they represented wealth and power. So, for a quality cut ruby, be expected to shell out a good $15,000! And that's just for one! And did you know that authentic rubies are rare to find? Yes, the authentic 100 percent ruby is rare to find.

Symbolically throughout biblical history, rubies also symbolized God's judgment, mercy, and righteousness. These are characteristics of God that execute His standards.

Doing Business As Unusual: Proverbs 31

In knowing these things about God, you know what to expect from Him.

So, what are some standards in your business' industry that are rare to find? And how would having that rarity shine the light on God and bring others closer to Him through your business?

What standard would you set for your business that many would pay good money just to have it? Take a minute to answer the question: what is a must-have for your business?

Comparisons to rubies are mentioned six times in the bible. This gem is seen as very precious and valuable. This is referenced to women as well as wisdom and knowledge.

In running your business, it should be considered as precious and valuable – not only in the services you offer, but also in the institution itself. Your business is a representative of you. What is your value as an individual? How do you see yourself, not only as an entrepreneur, but as a person? What is your level of integrity and purpose? Who do you reflect in your business? Your character and values are very important evaluation points. One thing about a business, is it is more than just making money and having freedom. It is about providing something for someone else, that by not having *it*, they would be incomplete without *it*.

What is the spiritual "price tag" that you've placed on your business and brand? When people come to you, are they viewing not only your products or services – but also you – as valuable? Are you rare and a must-have?

Seek to be virtuous. Structure in your business plan to have standards that are rare, yet precious, and highly valuable that no one can do without.

Proverbs 31:11-12

"The heart of her husband trusts in her, and he will have no lack of gain. She does him good, and not harm, all the days of her life." ESV

Can people trust you? Not only with their money, but with their needs? Can they trust that whatever product or service that you're offering them, it will actually solve a problem or meet a need – or are you using a smokescreen pretending that you care only to make a sale?

In these two scriptures, God wants us to be entrepreneurs of integrity. Whatever you speak out of your mouth, you are being held accountable to the people who hear it – whether you know them personally or not. Or whether you spoke it to them directly.

As an entrepreneur, you are to solve a problem – or meet a need. When people work with you, are they still going to be in lack? Are they going to be in more debt than before; because now they've spent money to still have the same issue?

In branding, you are expected to build a trust! People will not buy your product or service just because you look good or because it's so awesome. They buy what they trust. Have you ever thought about brands such as Wal-Mart? They are notorious for having some of the worst customer service ever – but they have developed a brand over the years that their products can be trusted. If you get it from Wal-Mart, you can trust it. It's not only convenient, but you can trust the products you receive from there to be exactly what you need, when you need it.

This scripture doesn't only apply to a woman's husband, but it applies to business partners as well as customers. These are the people who should be close and dear to your heart as an entrepreneur, because without them, you have no business!

When you start a business, you enter a relationship. You have various members – your partners, you employees or team, and your customers. A business ran God's way is a business that people can trust. Not only in word, but also in deed and service.

I like in verse 11, that the "husband" will have no lack of gain. That's powerful! Can you imagine the prosperity level in that?

Because of the trust factor, there is no lack. Evaluate the areas of your business where there is lack. What's missing? What is it that ether you don't trust or your customers don't trust about how you're running your business? Does God even trust your business? I suppose that should be the first question you ask.

When we understand the blueprint that God has laid out for us, we will start to see the increase. We will begin to reap the fruit of the connections that we've sown into over the beginning stages of our business development.

Becoming a business owner shouldn't only be about what we can do for ourselves. It should be about how we can help someone else. What can we return to them?

We should question ourselves and ask – do people trust me? Can they entrust their most vulnerable needs to what I have to offer? Whether it's content or information – authors

Doing Business As Unusual: Proverbs 31

and writers or tangible things, our business should be trustworthy. Those who are connected to us should be comfortable in placing their very essence in our hands, believing that their needs will be met – without lack.

Proverbs 31:13

"She seeks wool and flax, and willingly works with her hands." NKJV

Building a brand is hard work – I mean, really, it is hard work. When you see celebrities who have made it from the grassroots on up, you only see that flash, fame, and acclaim. But it takes had work to build your brand. It takes late nights, tears, sweat, money, disappointments, and abandonment to build a brand and business.

Usually when people quote Proverbs 31, not many mention or focus on verse 13. But let's examine it a little bit. Wool and flax were very important materials in biblical times. For men who travelled extensively, they needed garments to protect them during harsh weather.

Wool was also used as bedding, a place to sit, and has natural oils in its fibers that was used to protect the skin. The quality was considered superior to other materials used during those times.

Fine linen was made from flax, and was a material that was cultivated from the Egyptians. It was a tedious task to make linen from flax, which ranged from drying and deseeding the stalks to soaking and re-drying the fibers and then combing the threads to prepare for weaving.

Flax was also used to make torches and wicks for lamps. Using flax for light sources were very valuable to those who often went to battle.

A wise woman who runs her business or builds her brand by God's blueprint, looks for resources that are highly useful and needed. She doesn't just start a business or build a brand just to say she has one – she strategically does it with a purpose, and she seeks out to sell, promote, and work with things that she knows will be of value to her customers and her family.

She is also willing to put in the work! Oftentimes in our fast-paced world, we seek the easy way out. "Build a business in 7 days, write a book in 3 days, etc." – you get the picture. And many of us have probably done it or even offered it.

I'm not saying that these pitches are wrong or sinful, but we should be willing to put in the work. Do what needs to be done to make it happen – no matter the cost. If we are serious about standing out and being a Proverbs 31 entrepreneur for the long-haul, we have to be willing to do what it takes to be greater.

Make sure that the resources you gather not only are important and useful, but that they're relevant. For example, if I am a hairstylist and my customer-base is women who have skin conditions and need a stylist to create hairstyles that compliment them as well as protect their sensitive skin types, it wouldn't be relevant in selling the latest perms or scented hair creams, because in understanding my clientele, I know that those things would become irritants to their skin. Your resource should be an addition to solving the needs of your customers, as well as showing that you are willing to go the extra mile in providing for needs that are conducive to their overall happiness and well-being as your customer. And this does take work. Do the research, know what you're offering and who you're offering to. Make sure you know about the resources you're using and the platform you're providing it on. Don't take the easy way out. Do the work.

Proverbs 31:14

"She is like the merchants' ships; she bringeth her food from afar." KJV

The scripture compares a woman about doing her business God's way to a merchant ship. A merchant ship transports or carries passengers for hire. The merchant ship is important to the city, because it brings the necessities for everyday life: food, supplies, etc.

How important are you as an entrepreneur? How dependent are your customers are on you for what they need? Do they rely on what you have to offer?

In building your brand, it goes beyond just looking or being "different." Your brand should become a necessity. The specialty that you have should be something customers can't live without or can't function their business without. You should be indispensable to your customers. Your brand should be the go-to recommendation for meeting a particular need and solving a particular problem.

Another aspect of the scripture is that she brings her food from afar. How far are you willing to go to bring what your customers need to them? Are you willing to step out of your comfort zone to meet their needs?

As an entrepreneur doing things God's way, we should always strive to give our customers what they need, and go by any means that is in our power to get it done (Proverbs 3:27). Our clients should view us as being just that concerned about what they need. Not only should we be concerned about handling their immediate pain points, but we should always seek to find out how we can help them in other areas of their lives or their businesses.

Doing Business As Unusual: Proverbs 31

There are businesses who address needs from a holistic approach – caring for the whole person. That may not be your niche, but are there other areas that you can assist with, that you haven't taken the time to look into?

Going the extra mile does two things: (1) it shows that you care about your customers as people, not just as sales, and (2) it solidifies your relationship with your customer, building trust as well as credibility as an expert to knowing your customers.

Proverbs 31:15

"She gets up while it is still night; she provides food for her family and portions for her female servants." NIV

If you've been working your business, you already know it is not your normal 9-to-5 job where you clock in and clock out. There are times when you put in late hours and dedicate plenty of energy to making your business successful.

As a Proverbs 31 entrepreneur, you not only work late into the wee hours making sure you provide for your family, but also for the people who work for and with you. You are a nurturer and provider. You are dedicated to getting the job done, and for building your business.

A Proverbs 31 entrepreneur realizes that without their employees, team, networking and/or business partners, they can't have a successful business and brand. So she doesn't only work hard to provide for her family, but also for those that are connected directly with her business.

Some of the best-made plans are done late in the night. Working in the late night hours is not a badge of honor, but it is oft-times mandatory, because you've had time to detox from the busyness of your day. Your listening capacity to God's leading is clearer at late evening and at dawn.

It's during the "midnight hours" that you receive breakthroughs and can capitalize on the "fresh wind" that God provides in the stillness of the night.

This is not to say that we should overwork ourselves, but it is to state that we should take advantage of those moments when we are up late at night working. We should seek to hear from the Lord on how we can provide not only for ourselves and our families, but also for our customers and those connected to our business.

Proverbs 31:16

"She considereth a field, and buyeth it: with the fruit of her hands she planteth a vineyard." KJV

In this verse, we see that an entrepreneur that runs her business according to God's blueprint, is shrewd. She doesn't take the first deal that comes her way. She weighs a matter, and does her research.

Sometimes we may think we have to jump on the latest thing, app, opportunity, etc. just because it becomes available to us. But a Proverbs 31 entrepreneur is shrewd in how she handles business. She considers all the pros and cons before she buys, invests, or becomes connected to something.

And with the hard work she performs, she uses her money, time, and resources wisely and re-invests right back into her business. There's nothing wrong with treating yourself, but your business isn't a one-time hit wonder! You want your business to continue to grow. And for that to happen, you have to re-invest. The "B" part of verse 16 says *with the fruit of her hands she plants a vineyard*. How much are you investing back into your business with your return? If you had a $4,000 week, how much of that did you invest in upgrading that calendar management workflow that you know you need to help streamline your clients and leads better? What about investing in that certification that will put you in the know with a new circle of clientele? This is important. Investments add value to your business, and it creates a solid foundation for your brand, in that it helps you to manage the needs of your clients better.

And when you reinvest, don't place all of your seeds in one pot. Spread them around! Create multiple streams of income to help sustain you during seasons of drought in your business. You may want to invest into penny stocks and next week, invest from your check, money into affiliate marketing with a company that connects with your brand. Don't just make careful business purchasing decisions, but also create a blanket of security for your business to keep it growing.

Proverbs 31:17
"She dresses herself with strength and makes her arms strong." ESV

Entrepreneurship is not for the weak or faint at heart. It is a dog-eat-dog world, and if you aren't ready to run the footman, you sure can't be ready to run with the horses!

Strength comes not only in the form of physical ability to overpower or dominate, but it also comes in the form of being consistent and tenacious. When you have those moments of wanting to throw in the towel, your strength kicks in to energize and empower you to keep going.

A Proverbs 31 entrepreneur pushes past the painful moments when the launch didn't go as planned; when the people who said they would support you, are the first ones to throw mud to your brand; when you invested in a project that flopped, or when you are just so exhausted that you can't even think straight.

Strength first starts in the mind, then it comes through your conversation (to yourself as well as with others), and then through your actions. Protect your most delicate thing – your business – with strength. Cover it daily in prayer, wise counsel, and a passionate drive.

Doing Business As Unusual: Proverbs 31

Proverbs 31:18
"She perceiveth that her merchandise is good: her candle goeth not out by night." KJV

So you think, so you are. How do you view your business or brand? How do you view the products or services that you offer? Do you actually think that what you do is good? If you don't think it is, how do you expect someone else who doesn't know it in and out the way you do to think it is?

When you go into business, one of the questions you should ask yourself is this: is this profitable? Is this just a hobby to pass the time away, or am I really looking to making a living doing this? And will people see the value in this, so that I can actually profit from it?

That's a lot of questions, I know. But a Proverbs 31 entrepreneur asks these questions. And it's not just when they get started in running a business, but this should be done periodically along the journey.

A Proverbs 31 entrepreneur assesses her business and brand often. She asks herself – and even her customers, if what she's offering to them is bringing a profit to them.
And be conscious that the work doesn't end at just asking the question. Hard work is a principle that can't be stressed enough in this chapter! Give your all to doing what is necessary to take your business and brand to your next level.

Proverbs 31:19
"She layeth her hands to the spindle, and her hands hold the distaff." KJV

Proverbs 31 entrepreneurs oftentimes have to wear so many hats to run their business and keep it going. And in the midst of wearing those hats, you can become overwhelmed – and distracted.

And distractions can pull you off course, causing important things to drop through the cracks. So how can you grow an effective business when you have cracks in the foundation?

In biblical times, a distaff is a stick in which wool is wound on for spinning. Without it, it would be rather difficult to do the work of creating wool and flax. It is important – no, it's crucial – that your foundation is solid, and that you hold on to it. Staying focused is also staying determined.

In the midst of distractions and losses, you have to remain focused and determined to keep going and working with the same passion and fervor that you had when you got your first customer.

Spin through the struggles and snags that the entrepreneurial journey affords. When you're faced with being overwhelmed, go back to the foundation. Go back to your distaff and hold onto it tight and with determination, until you can spin back into the process.

Doing Business As Unusual: Proverbs 31

Proverbs 31:20
"She stretcheth out her hand to the poor; yea, she reacheth forth her hands to the needy." KJV

Philanthropy is something commonly associated with billionaires. Why? Not only because of the tax credits, but also because of the benefits of giving. God's principles are everlasting and sure, regardless of whether you're a believer in Him or not.

Ecclesiastes 11:1 says to cast thy bread upon the waters: for thou shalt find it after many days.

Malachi 4:10-11 says to bring all of your tithes into the storehouse, that there may be meat in mine house, and prove me now herewith, saith the Lord of hosts, if I will not open you the windows of heaven, and pour you out a blessing that there shall not be room enough to receive it. And I will rebuke the devourer for your sakes, and he shall not destroy the fruits of your ground; neither shall your vine cast her fruit before the time in the field, saith the Lord of hosts.

Luke 6:38 Give, and it will be given to you. A large quantity, pressed together, shaken down, and running over will be put into your lap, because you'll be evaluated by the same standard with which you evaluate others.

God's promises are sure; even in business. I like how in this scripture, it says she "stretcheth." When you're busy building your business on a minimal budget, it can be hard to give. But God wants us to give. He wants us to stretch ourselves, even in the small things.

Doing Business As Unusual: Proverbs 31

Investment for your business comes in many forms. It's not just about investing money, but it includes resources, time, and network… So, why is it important to share with the "poor"? First, the poor is not necessarily someone who is lacking in money, but it may be a colleague who is struggling to get a leg-up in their industry. And if you so happen to have a contact to assist them, then it is your mandate to sow a seed into them. We have to remember you can't put something in a closed fist. The poor can also mean that you have a lead that needs a particular service that your colleague can help, and you share that with them. It may also be information that can be useful in helping your customers. Give it to them; without cost. Sow into them, that you may reap referrals.

Be a confident Proverbs 31 entrepreneur. Because you believe God will honor His promises, you can be confident that what belongs to you is yours. There is no fear or uncertainty in sharing with others. Reach for others; meaning, looking forward to helping those in need. One of the greatest feelings, and rewards in the world is knowing that you can help someone else.

Proverbs 31:21

"She is not afraid of the snow for her household: for all her household are clothed with scarlet." KJV

Fear is always seen as a weakness and sin for Christians. And it presents conflict to us when we're faced with it, yet many times we try to ignore it. Fear is not a trait that pleases God, but He evaluates us by how we handle it.

God wants us to trust Him even in the times when we don't know the way. Jesus said He is the way, the truth and the life. Whenever we have a complicated decision to make in our business, Jesus says He is the way.

In situations of uncertainty, we are to look to the promises God has already given us. The snow of life can be debilitating and cause us to slow down in the process of success, but a Proverbs 31 entrepreneur will seek cover and comfort. Scarlet refers to the warmth and comfort. The snow in Palestine during biblical times came, but it was in small quantities and then soon disappeared.

Fear for a Proverbs 31 entrepreneur should be a tool of motivation. Do you remember WHY you wanted to become an entrepreneur? Fear comes as a stumbling block to not stop you, but to increase your strength for the journey; hold onto your WHY. Know this: you should expect the snow of life! Expect it, and be ready to get suited up for when it comes to walk through it. Your focus should always be to get things done, know that the snow is only for a season; it's only for a moment. Stay focused.

Proverbs 31:22
"She maketh herself coverings of tapestry; her clothing is silk and purple." KJV

As entrepreneurs, we can sometimes be so overwhelmed with running the business that our appearance may go to the back burner. But we have to remember that we are our brand. And at all times – we are representing our brand to potential clients.

A Proverbs 31 entrepreneur must be aware of how she presents herself when going to networking events, meetings, and client meetings. She glorifies God in her appearance – not in excess, but in showcasing that she is a woman that is serious about business and she is equipped to handle the task.

Be careful in making sure that you dress not only to impress, but to convey the right message. Choose materials, brands, colors, and styles that match your brand as well as connects with your audience. Did you know that certain clothing materials and colors symbolize "empowerment" and "leadership"? When you walk into a boardroom, what colors do most of the executive team wear? Have you ever paid attention to that?

The color blue exudes trust and confidence. Black is viewed as a color that communicates sophistication and to be taken seriously. While the color gray expresses a person who is self-sufficient and capable of handling their job.

In your attire choices, make sure you are modest – even with your royal and creative colors. Your royal colors, whether they are bold or eccentric colors, should always be "splashed" in your ensemble. They shouldn't overpower or dominate your outfit. A prime example is if you're wearing all black, splash it with a pink shell or scarf. Black is the power color, and if you're going for more subtlety and wear gray, you can always splash it with a baby blue or soft turquoise shirt under your jacket, or a dress pin. Remember that first impressions are lasting impressions. You want to make a statement, but you want your brand to show up before you do.

Proverbs 31:23
"Her husband is known in the gates, when he sits among the elders of the land." NASB

What you do doesn't only affect you, but it affects your family. Making good business decisions speaks volumes to people who know you on a personal level. It pays to make sound decisions, and exercise good business judgment; for you never know what deals are made on your behalf outside of the boardroom.

Your family is your first business, and they reflect your brand even when you're away from the office. People are always watching how you interact with your family, how you handle your spouse, etc. If a potential business partner sees that your husband isn't respected because of your unhealthy business practices, then they may be less willing to invest in working with your business.

Make it a priority to take care of home first. Make sure that your family conducts themselves in a manner that is pleasing and respectable. It is not an easy task, but it definitely worth the investment.

Entrust your husband as your first investor in your business. And make sure that he is familiar with your mission and your work. When others see him, they will connect him to the work that you do – and if it is good work, it will not only elevate you, but it will elevate him because of his association to you and your brand.

Proverbs 31:24
"She makes linen garments and sells them, and supplies belts to the tradesmen." NASB

A Proverbs 31 entrepreneur sees up the road. She knows the needs of her clients before they know they need it. She makes sure that whatever pain point they have, she does what is in her power to provide a solution. Even if she has to enlist outside support or resources, she does her due diligence in making sure her clients' needs are met.

A Proverbs 31 entrepreneur also believes in having more than one stream of income. She knows the needs of her first business (her family), and does what she needs to do to take care of them. Having a business does not always provide surety. So, in her wisdom, she knows she has to always have a plan B to sustain her two success. She strategically plans her other means of income, and she works diligently to make sure she uses her skills and talents wisely and for the edification of man and the glory of God.

A smart entrepreneur just doesn't invest in her income builders, but she also uses the investment to produce additional returns for her. In other words, she makes the linen, but she doesn't just use it to make clothes for her family, but she uses it to sell and bring a return profit to make more and to reinvest in her other businesses.

Having multiple streams of income is important in entrepreneurship. Yes, be the master of one, but also invest in more to generate a substantial and sustainable foundation for your business and brand. Let your gifts make room for you! (Proverbs 18:16)

Proverbs 31:25
"Strength and honor are her clothing; and she shall rejoice in time to come." KJV

This entrepreneurial journey is not for the faint at heart. It takes passion, dedication, motivation, and consistency. As an entrepreneur, it is important that you understand the process of growth and success. There is no cookie-cutter plan for success, nor is there an easy-route to being successful in 30 days or less.

The journey gets difficult and you may fail many times before you can even see the light of day in your business. But don't give up! You were designed for this kind of success.

Many are called to be entrepreneurs, but there are a few that are chosen to succeed as entrepreneurs, because they rely on their own strength and abilities. A Proverbs 31 entrepreneur leans not to her own understanding, but she falls to her knees in prayer and seeks the guidance of the Lord in her decisions. She builds and owns her business on the foundation of integrity and depends on the Lord to carry her through even the dark periods where no one is purchasing and supporting her business.

She leans to His understanding when the bills are due, but the income is short. She trusts His judgment when she has to re-invest her re-investment to shift her original plan for her business. And during her darkest hours, she still rejoices because she knows that God is with her, and the seeds she has sown into her business will soon manifest a harvest that she could not even imagine.

This kind of entrepreneur stands on the promises of God over her life, family, and her business. She trusts in what He planted, and although she may feel like she wants to give up, she doesn't, because her strength comes from the Lord to carry her through to the next level in what is destined for her.

Proverbs 31:26

"She opens her mouth in skillful and godly wisdom, and on her tongue is the law of kindness [giving counsel and instruction]." AMP

Can people trust what comes from your lips? Have they established a trust with you and your brand? Do you (your products) do what you say you're going to do?
As entrepreneurs, it is vital to honor your reputation. Don't just build a brand because it sounds good. Build it on the truth and the authenticity of your character.

And when you speak, people should be quick to listen to what you have to say, because of the value that you provide them. You should also be confident in what you know! Don't be timid in your expertise. Acknowledge and affirm it before your audience. You got the training, you experienced it, now you own it.

The thought process is that if you're going to be taken seriously as an entrepreneur, you have to have a hard-as-nails attitude and not allow yourself to be vulnerable and open to people. And to some extent, there is some truth to it. God doesn't want us to operate unwisely or without clarity. But He reveals to us in verse 26, that we are to speak with the law of kindness. We have to be willing to share resources, give kudos and celebrate others that are succeeding, and give encouragement when the Spirit of God gives us admonition.

Our brands/businesses should reflect God's character of compassion, respectfulness, and the desire to draw others; not only to our business, but also to Him. People can't see God, but they can see us. And if we are His, we should represent Him well.

Doing Business As Unusual: Proverbs 31

When we give advice, we should not be condescending and harsh – remember we were once new also! We made some of those same mistakes, and we had to learn along the way. Be clear, and don't sugarcoat, but have a spirit of kindness and desire that they succeed, just as you would want someone to cheer you on to success. Allow the law of kindness and wisdom to lead the way for you in your customer service toward colleagues and clients.

Proverbs 31:27
"She looks well to how things go in her household, and the bread of idleness (gossip, discontent, and self-pity) she will not eat." AMP

A Proverbs 31 entrepreneur has too much to do, and doesn't have time to gossip on the phone or on social media about who is doing "what" in their business. They have their own business to build! They don't have time to complain and grumble about how things are not going their way. They have too many ideas to try out and too many networking partners to collaborate with. And who has time to waste on self-pity? If you fail, dust yourself off and get back at it. The vision was given for free, but the work is going to cost you. It's going to cost you: fear, insecurity, doubt, and self-reliance.

You don't have the time to waste ingesting all of that negativity. All it's going to do is make you sick, and have you setting back on your purpose. You have a brand to establish, a business to run, and an empire to build! Your family is depending on you to leave a legacy; a seed for them to plant and nurture.

As an entrepreneur, time is a valuable resource. It is limited in the means that it is going to take all that you have and more to build your business successfully. So you have no time to waste on idleness. A Proverbs 31 entrepreneur may be delayed, but she isn't denied. Don't weigh yourself down with the weight of idleness. Get behind the scenes and work like there is no tomorrow. The time you waste being idle, is time you can be working on your comeback strategy. It's time you can be planning your next campaign. It's time you can be connecting with a queen that is going to take your empire to the next level. Remember, your time is like a rare jewel, and it should be handled wisely.

Proverbs 31:28
"Her children rise up and call her blessed; her husband also, and he praises her." ESV

How empowering is it to have your own personal cheerleading squad? It means a lot when you have a family who supports you and all of your hard work.

But the truth is, unfortunately, not everyone is going to support your vision. They aren't going to start off seeing you as an entrepreneur, because for so long they've gotten used to seeing you as an employee. Their mindset has not transitioned to the sacrifice and faith-walk of an entrepreneur. But just keep going! Keep moving forward and putting in the work.

God's word doesn't lie, and soon your family will be right there cheering you on! This is a major manifestation of all that you put into or invest into your business or brand. It is such a blessing to have children who recognize the sacrifices and effort you've put into building their legacy. And for them to one day see the manifestation, and declare you to be blessed – oh, that's such a wonderful accomplishment!

Don't give up. And in the meantime, surround yourself with people who are supportive to your success. Listen to wisdom and counsel after you have made a mistake, and make sure that counsel is looking out for your greater good. Accept the love and motivation that they give you. You can't walk this journey successfully alone! It takes a tribe or village to build a successful business, because they serve as your fuel to help you recharge. They speak into you (and declare over you) the love, encouragement, and tools to keep you moving forward.

Doing Business As Unusual: Proverbs 31

The praise is glory to God, but it testifies of your hard work for your business. It does not go unnoticed, and it will open doors for you to expand and grow.

Proverbs 31:29
"Many women have done excellently, but you surpass them all." ESV

My dear entrepreneurs, don't get into the bad habit of comparing yourself to another entrepreneur. Don't define your place and level of success to theirs. You are unique and one of a kind! God sees you in your journey as great and surpassing them all who try to be like you.

There is only one you, and your brand is unique and custom-designed for your skills, character, and abilities to attract and care for YOUR customers. Even if you're in the same business as another woman, your brand is still important, and different. Your responsibility is to go through this journey to find out what your "uniqueness" is.

That's why branding is so critical. It is what defines you from the rest. Search through your SCA (skills, character, and abilities) to connect the dots to your own brand. Even when someone sees your creativity and try to "steal" or copy it, you are still set apart. They may even gain from copying from you, but when you trust God with your brand, He transforms you and grows your business in ways that they can't imitate. You surpass all of the copycats with a brand that speaks to your audience only, and no one can replace that.

Proverbs 31:30
"Charm is deceitful and beauty is vain, but a woman who fears the Lord, she shall be praised." NASB

Remember when we talked about your appearance and making an impression? Well, we also have to make sure that the inside matches the outside. We can look like a million bucks, but be dead of motivation and success on the inside.

Your success begins inwardly. Your thoughts, feelings, character, etc. is what becomes a gauge of success to the Lord. He looks at our motives for wanting to succeed, and our heart's passion to the work we put in.

When we respect God's leading, God's blueprint, and His encouragement, others will see it and praise us – not in our own strength, but in how God moves so mightily on our behalf. Your reputation will proceed you, and people won't hesitate in wanting to work with you. They will be comfortable with your brand, and will look to your expertise and your brand for answers.

For example, if you are a caterer, people will see you as one who cares about what their food tastes like, their preferences, their health plan, and their goals for weight management or just changing their lifestyles! The testimonies will come and establish credibility with your brand among your potential clients and overall target audience. How you think will show on the outside in how you treat others' as well as how you react to their pain points. The great Maya Angelou once said, people will forget what you said, but people will never forget how you made them feel. Having a great brand, excellent office space, a snazzy business name, state-of-the-art equipment, and all of that means nothing if you don't have what matters on the inside.

Seek to do God's will, and to give Him the glory in your business. Seek to have compassion for your customers and treat them with the same respect and concern that you want from others. Seek to look not to others, but to the Lord's vision for your brand, and watch how He will open doors for you to prosper, and watch how those around you will testify of your character and the authenticity of your developing brand.

Proverbs 31:31

"Give her of the fruit of her hands, and let her works praise her in the gates." ESV

It is a wonderful feeling to see that your hard work is paying off – finally. It feels great to know that everything you've sacrificed and put into building even the smallest step upward has manifested.

This last chapter is about celebrating the victories. We all have high expectations for ourselves when we first go into business. We want to land the "ideal client," make that first 6-figure income, relinquish every care of the world by the product of our business, and so on. You get the point.

But we tend to forget the little victories along the way. We diminish the fact that we were able to accomplish painting the walls in our new office, to finally purchase new cooking equipment, getting the business plan done, or finally deciding on a name for your business! Celebrate the small things in your business, because yesterday, you didn't have them. Honor all of the work that you do because it matters. They are all pieces to building your empire.

A Proverbs 31 entrepreneur plants for, expects, and accepts a harvest. When people begin to see you celebrate yourself, they will in turn celebrate you. Let your own party of one catch fire and catch the attention of your next customer. They're waiting for a Proverbs 31 entrepreneur. They're waiting for you.

Sources & References:

• http://www.askgodtoday.com/2013/06/07/2-reason-its-more-precious-than-rubies/

• https://coaimhe.wordpress.com/2011/01/15/her-worth-is-far-above-rubies/

• http://www.addmorecolortoyourlife.com/gemstones/ruby.asp

• http://www.biblestudytools.com/commentaries/gills-exposition-of-the-bible/proverbs-31-13.html

• http://www.giveshare.org/BibleStudy/153.wool.html

• https://www.studylight.org/dictionaries/hbd/f/flax.html

• https://www.letgodbetrue.com/proverbs/commentaries/31_22.php

The complimentary book to Doing Business as Unusual...

Business Usually Makes Money

This is part two in this book's series for men who are looking to run and grow their business by God's principles.

Examine an example of Godly stewardship through two Godly men of honor.

Book coming soon!

Build your business with great resources.

UpWrite Solutions' Resource Library has eBooks, webinars, cheat sheets, and more just for you! Whether you are a new kid on the block, or looking to sharpen up your skills, the Resource Library has something for you.

Check out FREE and reasonably priced items today!

www.upwritesolutions.com/resource-library

ABOUT THE AUTHOR...

Tonya Franklin is from Mississippi, but has lived abroad in Europe. She has written and published three books, and owns her own virtual assistance business, UpWrite Solutions. She also owns the brand, *I Speak. To Empower*, which serves young girls ages 8-18 teaching and speaking topics of personal and spiritual development as well as women ages 19-50 on topics of business development and empowerment.

Tonya also is the Founding Manager of the brand *Books by Tonya* that serves as the headquarters for all of her books, as well as her marketing, training, speaking brands and services for media personnel, ministers, speakers, authors, writers, and coaches.

She loves cooking, crossword puzzles, and of course, reading and writing.

www.tonyadfranklin.com
www.payhip.com/booksbytonya

Connect with Tonya!

Facebook: @tonyathewriter
Twitter: @writeitright7
Instagram: @booksbytonya

Find her on Goodreads and Amazon!

www.ingramcontent.com/pod-product-compliance
Lightning Source LLC
Chambersburg PA
CBHW050029230526
45470CB00003B/1200